STRATEGIC SANITATION APPROACH

A review of literature

STRATEGIC SANITATION APPROACH

A review of literature

Darren Saywell and Andrew Cotton

Water, Engineering and Development Centre (WEDC)
GHK International Research & Training
UNDP-World Bank Regional Water and Sanitation Group (South Asia)

Water, Engineering and Development Centre,
Loughborough University,
Leicestershire, LE11 3TU, UK

© WEDC, Loughborough University, 1998

ISBN 13 Paperback: 978 0 90605 560 1
ISBN Ebook: 9781788533584
Book DOI: http://dx.doi.org/10.3362/9781788533584

A reference copy of this publication is also available online at:
http://www.lboro.ac.uk/wedc/publications/

WEDC (The Water, Engineering and Development Centre) at Loughborough University
in the UK is one of the world's leading institutions concerned with education, training,
research and consultancy for the planning, provision and management of physical
infrastructure for development in low- and middleincome countries.

This edition is reprinted and distributed by Practical Action Publishing.
Since 1974, Practical Action Publishing has published and disseminated books and
information in support of international development work throughout the world.
Practical Action Publishing trades only in support of its parent charity objectives and
any profits are covenanted back to Practical Action (Charity Reg. No. 247257, Group
VAT Registration No. 880 9924 76).

This document is an output from a project funded by the UK
Department for International Development (DFID)
for the benefit of low-income countries.
The views expressed are not necessarily those of DFID.

Designed at WEDC by Rod Shaw
Layout by Hallahan Chatterton

Contents

Glossary

Incentives: Factors that can stimulate behaviours required from different stakeholders. Incentives are said to be perverse when they are incompatible with goals of an enterprise or programme, including misdirected subsidies, unrealistic coverage targets, inappropriate career structures and credit restrictions on the poor.

Investment efficiency: Success in seeking investment from governments, donors, private finance institutions.

Operational efficiency: Allowing resources to go further and extending sanitation coverage.

Unbundling: Unbundling is a way of dividing investments into more realistic and manageable components. These separate components can be relatively independent or linked so that performance of one is dependent on that of others. *Horizontal* unbundling refers to the way in which services in different areas are provided by different organisations and/or in different ways. *Vertical* unbundling refers to the way in which services at different levels in a hierarchical system are provided by different suppliers.

Acronyms

CBO	Community Based Organisation
CDC	Community Development Council
CVM	Contingent Valuation Method
DFID	Department for International Development
DSC	Development Support Communication
GoI	Government of India
IUID	Integrated Urban Infrastructure Development
LBD	Locally Based Demand
MM	Mahila Milan
MSIP	Multi Sector Investment Planning
NGO	Non-Governmental Organisation
NSDF	National Slum Dwellers Federation
O&M	Operation and Maintenance
OPP	Orangi Pilot Project (Pakistan)
RWSG	Regional Water and Sanitation Group
SIP	Slum Improvement Project
SPARC	Society for the Promotion of Area Resource Centres
SSA	Strategic Sanitation Approach
UBSP	Urban Basic Services Programme
UWSS	Urban Water Supply and Sanitation
WASA	Water and Sanitation Agency
WSSCC	Water Supply and Sanitation Collaborative Council
WSS	Water Supply and Sanitation
WTP	Willingness to Pay

Local terms

Nullah	Open drain

Part A
Introduction

Abstract

This document reports findings from Phase 1 of a Department for International Development (DFID) funded project (R6875) concerning the development of practical guidelines for the application of the Strategic Sanitation Approach in urban areas. Results from a review of literature are discussed.

A total of 63 documents were examined in the review and discussion has been summarised according to the key chapter headings used in Albert Wright's publication *Towards a Strategic Sanitation Approach*. The review also draws on an interview with key DFID personnel involved in projects in India (Lucknow, Cochin, Cuttack).

The purpose of the review is to examine how the key concepts underlying the Strategic Sanitation Approach (SSA) have been addressed in operational terms on the ground, highlighting examples where SSA ideas have been applied, what problems were identified in their application, and what issues require further consideration or clarification with the approach as a whole. Each section ends by abstracting the key points identified and posing questions which remain unresolved.

WEDC is part of the project team which is led by Kevin Taylor of GHK Research and Training, and includes Barbara Evans of the UNDP-World Bank Regional Water and Sanitation Group (South Asia). Their comments on the review are gratefully acknowledged.

Part B:
Literature review

Publications reviewed

The review was widespread covering a range of themes identified in the Strategic Sanitation Approach, as developed by Albert M Wright. SSA's principles have been described directly or indirectly in just a few published documents, including Wright (1997), UNDP-World Bank Water and Sanitation Group RWSG - South Asia (1997), Simpson-Hebert and Woods (1997), and Saidi-Sharouze (1994). Similarly, only a few publications were found to deal specifically with the application of the whole approach; in most cases literature discussed how key elements of SSA had been used.

The review begins with a concise overview of the approach (see An introduction to SSA), highlighting the core elements Wright (1997) defined in his key work, *'Towards a Strategic Sanitation Approach: Improving the Sustainability of Urban Sanitation in Developing Countries'*. This review adopts a broadly similar structure to that found in Wright's work. However, the section relating to 'Adopting a strategic sanitation approach' is not covered explicity, since these points are covered within other parts of the review. Each section begins with a summary from Wright's document, and then proceeds with a review of literature relevant to this point.

A list of references consulted in the literature review can be found in the Appendix.

Methodology

The review was physically conducted both in the UK (at WEDC) and in India (at the offices of the UNDP-World Bank Regional Water and Sanitation Group in New Delhi).

In the UK, a mix of document types were searched at the WEDC Resources Centre, including published project reports, books, academic and professional journals, conference papers and grey literature sources. Additionally, electronic databases were reviewed using keywords to collate relevant references for inclusion in the review (databases consulted included: Compendex (1994-98); Science Citation Index (1994-98); Social Science Citation Index (1990-98); BIDS ISI; Applied Science and Technology Abstracts; Applied Social Sciences Index and Abstracts; ASCE's Civil Engineering Database and Geobase (1990-1998)).

A range of document types were also reviewed at RWSG's offices in New Delhi.

The Strategic Sanitation Approach

An introduction to SSA

The Strategic Sanitation Approach (SSA) was developed by the UNDP-World Bank Water and Sanitation Programme and is built on examples from its own experience, World Bank work in the sphere of urban development and others' practice in the sector worldwide.

The need to rethink the approach to urban sanitation interventions in developing countries was a response to the unsatisfactory performance of past approaches which typically led to over-reliance on supply driven approaches, neglect of user requirements, emphasis on large scale projects which restricted competition and bundled together costs, and poor attention to O&M of installed systems.

Although strategic sanitation planning has been described in its application in two West African cities (Saidi-Sharouze, 1994), Wright (1997) provides the most comprehensive definition and review of the approach, explaining that the goal of SSA is to achieve the *sustainable* expansion of sanitation coverage in urban areas. SSA's emphasis on sustainability addresses a key problem of past supply driven approaches, that of focusing unduly on coverage statistics rather than long term O&M. Investment efficiency (defined as success in seeking investment from governments, donors, private finance institutions) and operational efficiency (defined as allowing resources to go further and extending coverage) are seen as prerequisites to obtaining this desired sustainability.

The approach differs from the existing supply driven agenda through two underlying principles: it is demand based, and incentive driven. A demand based approach relies on agencies conducting effective demand assessment exercises, and on thorough stakeholder participation. A key challenge for governments and agencies is to motivate and build capacity of different actors to participate in appropriate and productive ways. The second underlying principle is that incentives can stimulate specific behaviours required from key actors to achieve sustainable expansion of sanitation coverage. The right incentives package (with appropriate rules, referees and rewards) can assist governments or municipal agencies achieve their primary goal.

The approach involves:

- **Wider choices concerning technologies and service levels**: including comprehensive information about technologies, support in determining appropriate levels of service, and flexibility in applying appropriate technologies and service levels within the wider context of municipal sanitation programmes;

- **Step by step actions**: sanitation systems need to be disaggregated, or 'unbundled' both vertically and horizontally. Horizontal unbundling may involve the replacement of centralised systems with decentralised systems which can be managed separately. It can also involve the adoption of different sanitation technologies in different areas. Vertical unbundling requires that hierarchically integrated systems are broken down into separate but technically integrated systems with responsibility for the design and subsequent management of facilities at different levels devolved to the most appropriate level (i.e., household, community, city);

- **Economic replication**: an economic goal of SSA is the full recovery of investment, operations, and maintenance costs, including financing and transaction costs;

- **Responsive institutional arrangements**: links between institutions need to be developed to allow users to participate in the decision making process and management of services within the context of the overall municipal sanitation programme.

In conceptual terms, the approach seeks to integrate social, technical, institutional and economic factors that have an impact on the sustainability of service provision. SSA is built on the key assumption that the provision of sustainable sanitation to urban areas is only possible by a demand oriented service delivery system, which implies a system that has the flexibility to offer alternative technological options and corresponding institutional arrangements for service delivery. The approach also encourages a wide view of sanitation services to the city as a whole, rather than stand alone projects for target communities or for a specific service. The importance of financial policies (at community and agency level) and emphasis on incentives (to perform) for various actors in all stages of the process of service provision, including construction, financing and maintenance, are stressed.

SSA is designed to be flexible enough to adjust to different regions and contexts, and to learn and apply lessons from new experiences. It has already been put to use successfully in planning sanitation interventions in several countries, with documented results in Ouagadougou, Burkina Faso; Conarky, Guinea; and a pilot project that covers 10 per cent of the city of Kumasi in Ghana.

Distinctive features

What makes the SSA distinctive from previous approaches is its emphasis on two principles: demand based approaches (which require stakeholder participation) and the use of incentives to shape behaviour (both institutional and personal, requiring rules, referees and rewards - the 3 R's).

Stakeholder participation

A central element of the SSA is that through consultation involving all stakeholders, common goals in a sanitation programme can be defined. The challenge for governments and donors is to provide an environment in which different stakeholders are able and willing to participate in suitable ways towards achieving a common goal. Urban residents may understand more than others the difficulties of inadequate sanitation, but they may be excluded from participating in the process of developing solutions, because they lack trust in local government / municipal agencies, or fear sanctions arising from their formal recognition. Women, as the main users and managers of sanitation services, are vulnerable to exclusion from this process, a factor which may diminish the sustainability of installed facilities (Wright, 1997).

The participation of communities in the development process has become a critical element in contemporary project design and management, and in some cases, project financing is conditional on the application of participatory processes (Plummer, 1998).

A critical part in the approach in relation to participation is the assertion that "...the challenge for governments and donor agencies is to motivate and build the capacity of different stakeholders to participate in appropriate and productive ways". (Wright, 1997: 11). It is notable that SSA fails to give details as to how stakeholder participation is to be initiated and developed. This failure is symptomatic of much of the discussion surrounding participation; it is a concept currently much in favour, is frequently recommended in project design, but a clear understanding of what constitutes meaningful and effective participation remains elusive (Abbot, 1996), as does guidance on how to make the concept work in practice (UNCHS/CityNet, 1997).

Much of the literature on this subject divides into two streams, that detailing lessons learnt from attempts at enabling stakeholder participation and building partnerships, and secondly, analysis of conditions required for building effective participation.

It is clear from the literature that the notion of partnerships is currently very fashionable within the WSS sector, and partnerships between government, private sector, and CBO's are seen to be particularly attractive. But the approach is not easy and if any party is not well informed it can end in disappointment and failure. Successful partnerships rely on clear and common areas of interest. An irony of the current emphasis placed on partnerships and wider stakeholder participation is that many stakeholders who form partnerships may actually be rivals for resources. In order for stakeholders to work in partnership with other agents, there is a need for a clear mandate and appropriate levels of skill training for key personnel (Davidson, 1996).

There are several project based examples which draw key lessons to be learnt about stakeholder participation.

Experience in fostering and sustaining urban partnerships for the provision of infrastructure in Ahmedabad, India indicate two basic lessons: that it is necessary to adopt both a broad focus in the scope of work undertaken (i.e., working directly with the poor and women who are the majority users of urban services) and an interlinked focus by fostering partnerships between key stakeholders such as CBO's, NGO's and Ahmedabad Municipal Council. (Mahila Housing Trust, 1997). These points are further developed by Delhi Action Group and Mahila Housing Trust (1997) who argue that although partnerships between stakeholders may start at the city wide level, there is a need for them to quickly decentralise to the level of the community in order to maintain motivation and enthusiasm in participation. This notion of decentralisation has parallels with the identification of incentives for stakeholders to participate. In the Bombay and Bangalore latrine construction programmes, the process of developing community participation was found to be simpler by focusing on those infrastructure items which communities feel to be most vital to their survival, which they can organise themselves and which will increase their confidence and capacity to deal with other

8

stages of service improvement (Kurup, 1997). Orangi Pilot Project (OPP) in Karachi, Pakistan had a similar emphasis on concentrating on the one issue of prime importance to the community (Hasan, 1992).

The same programme identified that negotiation with the municipal corporation authorities (over service provision) could and should be conducted by the community (Kurup, 1997). This introduces an interesting area of discussion within the literature, that of the interface between different stakeholders. For OPP, a primary project constraint was the problem of integrating two key stakeholders with different defining characteristics (i.e., the formal/rigid procedural nature of local authorities, and the relatively more flexible and dynamic nature of community based organisations) (Siddiqui and Rashid, 1997). The activities of local authorities as institutions are typically constrained by factors including the lack of legislative or administrative authority, limited political support, inappropriate organisational structure, skills, staff or systems to effectively integrate participation into the process of delivering infrastructure services. To compound this situation, many local authority officials may fail to accept or misperceive the role and value of community participation in what was previously the domain of technical staff. Recent DFID research funded on how local government promotes and responds to participation in planning has identified several broad subject areas which limit the potential for successful participation. These focus on the impact of unsupportive politico-legal structures, inflexible ways of working at the municipal level, insufficient capacity within local government and perceived limitations of municipal staff towards working with the urban poor in participatory ways (Plummer, 1998).

This breakdown in working relationships between stakeholders may be addressed in several ways. A 'locally based demand' (LBD), implies a fundamental reorientation in the way governments and service organisations do business, seeking to alter the relationship between all stakeholders. One of the key advantages of the approach is its emphasis on forums which include officials, ministers, technical staff and communities which allow these different actors to come into direct contact, thereby helping to overcome stereotyped perceptions of each other (Varley et al, 1996). However, studies relating to the impact of such approaches on promoting stakeholder participation are limited. Paul (1996) and the Foundation for Public Interest (FPI) (1997) are exceptions to this rule, both reviewing the use of 'report cards' on cities, a tool to enable wider stakeholder participation through the assessment of public services for the poor. The report card exercise focused on Ahmedabad,

Pune and Bangalore case studies where poor urban residents are able to participate in the management of their city using consultations to identify the facilities most commonly used, levels of satisfaction with those services and analysis of the problems that are specific to each facility.

It is not just with local authorities that difficulties are experienced in building effective stakeholder participation. Manikutty (1997) discusses user participation and emphasises the importance of maintaining transparency in participation processes, otherwise there is a risk that community participation may become dominated by elites. Mechanisms to overcome the dominance of elites include ensuring that procedures for decision making at the local level are transparent, such as open public meetings, and opportunities to appeal against decisions. If local democratic institutions are in place and operational, these need to be integrated into the process. Encheverri-Gent (1992) argues that established elites within a community are typically too entrenched to be displaced, and that community participation becomes one more vehicle for domination. Desai (1996) has discussed similar themes in relation to participation in slum upgrading and improvement projects in Bombay. She suggests that 'community leaders' tend to come from local elites and tend to have better access to politicians and bureaucrats than ordinary slum dwellers. They gain considerable power through the patronage that they are able to exert by virtue of their position and the fact that they provide the only route through which slum dwellers can gain access to government authorities. Van der Linden (1997) discusses the role of patronage in inhibiting solutions to housing and infrastructure problems in the Sindh province of Pakistan. He argues that those who benefit by providing patronage have a vested interest in ensuring that systems and procedures remain obscure. This is an important issue in relation to the need for clear rules, referees and rewards identified by the SSA. These aspects of the debate about the nature of the urban 'community' are poorly explored in the SSA, but they are fundamental to any understanding of a 'community based' approach. Communities are rarely uniform, but are a mixture of ethnic / socio-economic / religious groups who will respond in many different ways to a common issue. As such, discussion of 'community based' approaches need to recognise this diversity.

In the Gajabapur Bosevana case study from Sri Lanka, two particular factors were found to enable participation of different stakeholders in the development process. Firstly, information sharing was a key aspect to mobilisation - the legal/technical issues of urban sanitary facilities, construction details of sewer lanes etc. were explained simply and clearly, in the local language, through an intermediary NGO (SEVANATHA) in participatory action research workshops. A second factor was the understanding that people's perceptions of urban sanitation are different from those of planners. Traditionally, planners looked at the macro perspective, while the people viewed developments from the micro or family level. Hence, people's participation was found to be higher if they are able to see some immediate benefit within the family or neighbourhood level. This second finding explained the reason why in the case study community mobilisation focused around family groups who became responsible for the maintenance and management of their own manhole in the localised shallow sewerage system (Hewawasam et al, 1997). Similar arrangements have been reported in various OPP publications. There must be some doubt about the efficacy of such arrangements in that the effects of a failure to maintain a particular manhole are not necessarily felt immediately by the people who live close to that manhole. Experience with condominial sewerage in Brazil suggests that there can be difficulties in organising regular ongoing maintenance through community organisations (Watson, 1995). While some neighbourhood associations do organise maintenance activities , either mobilising efforts by residents themselves or collecting money so that plumbers can be hired, public agencies are said to be by far the most common third-party maintenance providers.

SSA assumes that stakeholder agencies are willing to participate towards the common goal of achieving a sustainable sanitation programme. Experience from the field, in particular the management of the Gomti River Pollution Control Project suggests that in Lucknow this idea was over-ambitious (Harvey, 1996). The relevant lesson learnt was that participation in a partnership depends on roles, responsibilities and expected outputs being defined and included in project memoranda. This needs to be clearly stated so that an organisation knows what is expected of it before committing itself to the project (UNCHS/CityNet, 1997). Recent research into the processes involved in building municipal capacity for community participation (GHK R&T, 1998) suggests the need to convince members of organisations at all levels, particularly at the top, of the benefits of participatory approaches. The research further suggests that this will only be achieved if they see ways in which the adoption of participatory approaches help them to achieve their own goals which may relate to improved financial performance and reduction in user complaints among others. This finding would appear to tie in with the SSA's stress on the importance of incentives.

11

The second stream of literature on this subject emphasises the conditions required to bring about effective and meaningful stakeholder participation. The Urban Basic Services Programme (UBSP) in India is essentially a strategy for community development through empowerment of people. The key elements of the strategy are fostering community mobilisation through formation of neighbourhood groups and co-ordinating 'convergence' of a range of programmes specifically targeted at the poor (Mehta, 1993). Its basic aim is to improve the reach of different schemes and on-going programmes for the poor in urban settlements. Convergence recognises that planning for the poor cannot be a separate exercise from overall planning in the city. UBSP's emphasis on convergence clearly overlaps with SSA's idea of providing an enabling environment for different stakeholder participation. Mehta provides some guidance on how the process of convergence was handled in the cases of Nasik and Aligarh, with the key elements of the convergence process including:

- Commitment of higher levels of government to the process was a prerequisite;

- Departmental guidelines to support the organisation of services were issued by the appropriate level of government;

- Personal interest of concerned local government officials is extremely important (advocacy workshops and informal committee structure to initiate co-operation are ways of maintaining interest);

- Because of high staff turnover in government ranks, it proved essential to develop advocacy literature and operational guidelines which explained the basic principles of UBSP, its potentials, constraints and some case studies of how it had worked.

Other methods are more conceptual. 'Development Support Communication' (DSC) is a tool designed to improve urban management by creating more efficient flows of information between stakeholders and by creating the institutional structures which facilitate communication between different urban actors. The objectives of DSC, including the improvement of institutional functioning at horizontal levels, encouragement of private / community sector participation in urban sector projects, and promoting local government understanding of other actors in the sector, clearly coincide with SSA's emphasis on widening participation. The main impact

12

of DSC is that it stimulates amongst urban planners and managers a more detailed picture of people's needs and potentials, which it achieves through an emphasis on fostering collaboration, open consultation between various sector agencies, and a range of participatory techniques such as group meetings, door to door visits, theatre and folkloristic media (Steinberg, 1996).

Most commentators assume that stakeholder participation is best achieved through some form of community organisation. An important issue is the optimum size of such organisations. One strongly supported viewpoint is that community organisations should be small, not representing more than about 50 households at the most. This approach is adopted in the OPP (Hasan, 1992) and for the Community Development Councils (CDC's) in Sri Lanka (UNCHS, 1993 p12). The reasoning is that only such small organisations can have a chance of truly representing community wishes and concerns. Where necessary, larger organisations can be formed through a federation of smaller organisations. However, there is some evidence that such small groups are difficult to sustain. The experience of the Faisalabad Area Upgrading Project (FAUP) in Pakistan is that larger 'neighbourhood' groups are more likely to persist and have a greater chance of successfully interacting with line agencies and local government (Tayler, 1997a). Regardless of this, there is evidence that attempts to devolve responsibilities to community organisations without sufficient preparation and agreement on roles and responsibilities can fail. An example is provided by the experience of rural water supply and sanitation in Pakistan (Zaidi, 1997).

The issue of assessing the quality of participation is not adequately covered in the literature. One method of assessing the effectiveness and quality of these partnerships is suggested, based on 'city wide' ratings (in terms of efficiency and poverty impact) and 'operational ratings' (service and project cycle) (Delhi Action Group and Mahila Housing Trust, 1997).

Key points:
- Stakeholder participation relies on urban partners sharing a common goal/vision, and having clearly defined and expressed roles, responsibilities and outputs;

- Incentives for participation need to be identified early in project design for different stakeholders;

13

- The interface, or points at which different stakeholders interact, are critical to engendering wider stakeholder participation. The institutional arrangements and working culture of local government can conspire against effective communication between partners;

- Forums, consultations etc. are simple but effective ways in which stakeholders can learn about other partner agencies. Information sharing, and mechanisms to facilitate communication need to be given a high priority;

Key questions:

- The participatory processes implied by stakeholder participation are alien to many local authority organisations. How can the vested interests of certain partners be overcome to achieve a coherent alignment of goals?

- How is it possible to shift resources in municipal authorities from 'back room' functions to 'front line' functions that directly serve and interact with other stakeholders? (Delhi Action Group / Mahila Housing Trust, 1997);

- Learning from mistakes ('Golden Booboos' (Kurup, (1997)) is one way of allowing lessons from participation to be reinvested in the subsequent process of learning. How many times should a stakeholder (i.e., the community) be allowed to make the same mistakes?

- Do all stakeholders have equal knowledge about the programme which they are expected to participate in? Is it understood equally by different groups (men/women; ethnic groups; 'rich' and 'poor')? Do methods of applying for sanitation programmes (such as written format, method and timing of payments) favour one group over another? (WSSCC, 1997)

- 'Communities' are rarely uniform. Who is the community that is involved in water and sanitation projects and how are these community members identified?

Incentives and the 3 R's

Incentives, factors that can stimulate behaviours required from different stakeholders, are central to achieving sustainable expansion of sanitation coverage. They typically involve the promise of rewards (financial or personal (such as distinction, prestige) or the threat of sanctions and penalties (i.e. such as for failure to pay bills on time). By devising a series of incentives that ensure investment and operational efficiency, governments and municipalities can provide an enabling environment in which to achieve sustainability.

The mechanism to achieve this is based on:

* **Rules** - which govern interactions within and between enterprises;

* **Referees** - who review behaviour and, where appropriate, administer rules;

* **Rewards** - (and sanctions) - for rewarding compliance, and penalising digression of, rules.

The key challenge is to ensure that each of the 3 R's is reflected in the institutional framework inherent in the sanitation intervention and that the effect of all three is consistent with the goals of strategic sanitation. The 3 R's above need to produce incentives which encourage widespread and appropriate stakeholder participation throughout the project; competition and involvement of the private sector; transparency and accountability; decentralised management; and optimum cost recovery by developing a sense of ownership amongst users (Wright, 1997).

Much of the literature recognises the key role to be played by appropriate incentives in sanitation programmes, without providing clear examples of how incentive packages have been implemented, or describing their impact. EHP (1997) describe the design of a sanitation programme for the urban poor in Montego Bay, Jamaica and identify the lack of incentives for households to buy into sanitation improvements as one of the common deficiencies of sanitation programmes in general, yet fail to provide detail about the types of incentives missing or those needed to rectify this problem.

However, examples of how incentives have been introduced to project plans can be cited. The work of the World Bank / GoI (1997) on urban water supply and sanitation is one case where details are described. The workshop report, having reviewed lessons learnt from its participants, argues for an incentive based enabling strategy to help redress the key problems faced in urban water supply and sanitation. This strategy is based on three key elements: democratic decentralisation, commercialisation of UWSS providers/private sector participation, and market oriented financial systems. Furthermore, 'systemic changes' (devolution of responsibilities to municipalities, separation of policy/regulatory functions from operation, introduction of competition to enable performance assessment) are cited as key additional elements in achieving this incentive based approach.

In Nepal, the Dhulikhel Water Users Committee linked incentives with sanctions. The project established a key requirement that households invest in toilets before a tap connection would be made. By linking service provision to eligibility requirement the project provides a clear expressed incentive for the user to respond to. However, the success of the scheme was found to depend on the existence of high demand for the first service (i.e., the toilet) and a procedure in which external intervention be withheld if key criteria were not met. Although some problems over enforcement were reported in this case, it was observed that the combination of sanction and reward had resulted in improvements to sanitary conditions (RWSG-South Asia, 1997).

An interesting issue arising from this study is the impact on the effectiveness of incentives of organisation size and proximity to the user. The Dhulikhel Water Users Committee indicates that a small, user controlled organisation can be relatively effective in basic service provision because there is an immediacy of contact between those providing the service and those using the service. This has the effect that problems and constraints which are noted are dealt with quickly and decisively. For the committee, the incentive was in avoiding potential loss of revenue, and for the user it was clear that defaulting would not be tolerated by the committee, nor by the wider community (RWSG-South Asia, 1997). A key lesson identified from this example is that organisations can only apply sanctions and incentives if it is given legitimacy by the people it aims to serve.

Although these examples point to specific components found in incentive packages, a critical point is that incentives are context specific, and will be difficult to generalise between projects. However, Evans (1995) in work on institutional incentives and the provision of urban sanitation provides a broad subject framework in which appropriate incentives are likely to be identified and required. These include the prevailing work cultures and organisations of executive agencies; the career paths of municipal officers; the relationship between municipalities and contractors for provision of infrastructure; the political environment in relation to sanitation infrastructure provision and the nature of the community being served itself.

In the Sri Lankan Gojapura-Bosevana case study simple project rules were developed by small family groups and community development councils (CDC) which governed the procedure of infrastructure provision (Jayaratne and Hewawasam, 1997). These rules included:

- First come, first served;

- No materials would be distributed until the community development council (CDC) had complete payment from the small group in question;

- Small groups should find the labour for construction themselves and pay for it directly;

- Any complaints should be made during the construction process;

- Construction of private toilets and connections to the main sewer was a family responsibility.

A key challenge for the SSA approach is the need to ensure that incentives (and by default the 3 R's) are reflected in the institutional framework governing sanitation interventions. Many projects promote structured learning in their project design, but few have actively adopted a learning culture, primarily because of strong institutional/cultural barriers to learning. RWSG - South Asia (1996) discuss how structured learning in project design can be used as a mechanism for achieving the incentive driven approach. Adaptive project design is viewed as a key feature. Although clear sets of rules and procedures can be laid down to guide implementation, the project needs to be designed so that lessons from earlier project phases can be fed back into the system. Key features on what a learning process within a project involves include:

- Define project rules as they exist on the ground, rather than as implementers would like them;

- Determine the rationale for project rules: be clear about what incentives these rules are meant to create and what the expected outcomes are;

- Having decided on indicators of assessment, analyse field results and link to project rules;

17

- Modify project rules;

- Document and disseminate results.

The key difference between structured learning and more traditional monitoring and evaluation is that the former takes field results from early phases and consistently collates/analyses findings so the project can improve. In this mechanism, project rules become the framework for learning.

The use of 'report cards' as applied to Ahmedabad, Pune and Bangalore in India give some indication of how incentives can be identified, with a view to incorporation into project design. A report card is an assessment tool by which citizens can participate in the management of their city, using consultations to identify the facilities most commonly used by the poor, levels of satisfaction with those services and assessing the problems that are specific to each urban service (Paul, 1996; Foundation for Public Interest (FPI),1997). By measuring the urban poor's levels of satisfaction/ dissatisfaction with public services provided by the municipality (i.e., in relation to issues such as 'availability of service'; 'use of service'.), the tool helps to clarify incentives for participation in infrastructure provision from the users perspective.

Key points:

- To an extent, incentives are intuitive features of project design and management, which may not be formalised. As a consequence, clear, well documented examples of the operation and impact of incentives structures are difficult to identify;

- The efficacy of incentives may be heightened in circumstances where service providers are familiar with user communities. This raises the idea that incentives structures may be easier to implement in highly unbundled systems;

- Incentives are context specific, and may be difficult to abstract between projects. Incentives ideally need to be differentiated by target groups - what acts as an incentive to one community may not equally apply to another;

18

Lessons of perverse incentives

Perverse incentives refer to those behaviours which are incompatible with the goals of a programme. They might include misdirected subsidies, inappropriate career structure paths, credit limitations imposed on the poor and institutional barriers to stakeholder participation. Corrective action will need to be applied in each case to ensure that the incentives no longer act in a perverse way.

An example of perverse incentives might include bureaucratic inflexibility, in which public enterprises have little incentive to improve performance. The result is poor economic efficiency, and poor orientation to consumer needs (Wright, 1997).

The reason that perverse incentives persist is that there is no motivation for individuals concerned with urban sanitation to address them (Evans, 1995). The emphasis in literature on perverse outcomes tends to concentrate on the institutional level, and relate to the culture, practices and motivation of government, municipalities and contractor relationships. Typical examples of perverse incentives include:

- Political imperatives may lead to government serving the most articulate or powerful groups within a community;

- Where regional and urban government are dependent on central government for annual budget allocation, there are incentives to maximise the budget and ensure that it is spent. This may lead to selection of projects which are relatively easy and quick to complete, rather than those which are most needed;

19

- Municipal officers attempting to minimise personal professional risk and discomfort;

- Emphasis laid on completion of physical works rather than operational works;

- Payment of 'speed money' (i.e. bribes) in order to quicken transactions between residents and public agencies over provision of urban services;

- Collusion between government officials and contractors over the process of awarding engineering contracts;

This ultimately leads to a division of responsibility and an institutional structure which produces incentives that are skewed away from the benefits of the community as a whole, and in particular, the poorest groups.

Perverse incentives can also be found to operate at community level. The development of informal and indigenous organisational forms (for example, chiefs, elders, slum lords) which have evolved over time to assist in the functioning and operation of a society, are typical features in many urban communities. These groups exercise different levels of authority and power within a community and have the potential to influence community decision making and the process of change in both a positive and negative manner. Local power structures can act to adversely affect the promotion of sanitation (Cotton and Saywell, 1998). In Accra, Ghana, local NGO's found that particular assemblymen (representatives of the municipal assembly at the local level) were found to be subverting NGO procedures and practices in the implementation of a VIP latrine scheme to suit their own agendas; in effect, acting from a perverse incentive.

A conceptual approach to addressing the problems of perverse incentives is offered by Wunsch (1991). In a paper considering institutional reorganisation as a means to improving performance, the idea that the best way to counter administrative under performance is through the organisation as the unit of analysis, is challenged. Organisation level interventions were found to be both too blunt and too generalised: too blunt to construct an incentive structure and too generalised in that it might lead to problems for other tasks which required different incentive structures. Wunsch advocates a revised approach in which the role of the individual in good/service production is emphasised. This individual oriented focus would seek to analyse specific

20

tasks needed to be performed to achieve a given goal, and would carefully evaluate the incentives and disincentives that were in place for people to take these actions.

How then to design institutions which create organisations which avoid the problems of perverse incentives? Institutional analysis (or Howard's 'diagnostic study' (1996)) attempts to systematically determine what sorts of good/ services require what sort of institutional arrangements. To achieve this requires conceptual frameworks which help analyse and link goods, tasks, incentive structures and rules. Institutional analysis will also have a role in studying the rules in use which organise and regulate (or fail to do so) the production/consumption of a good or service. Assuming that the actors are unchanging, institutional analysis looks to manipulate the rules surrounding and affecting the conjunction between producers/consumers and the good/ service. Whilst this is theoretically possible, it should be stressed that the local political and administrative realities will determine the nature and extent of any possible corrective action to redress perverse incentives.

Key points:

- Perverse incentives can arise from a diverse number of sources (i.e. personal, professional, political). Once established, it is difficult to break down regimes which are designed to serve vested rather than collective interest;

- Some form of systematic review or analysis of stakeholders is required in order to gain an entry point into the motivations and procedures which underline perverse incentives;

- Corrective action needs to address two separate issues, initially the reasons why perverse incentives arise, and consequently, the factors which help to sustain such outcomes;

- Corrective action needs to be focused through the individual as the primary unit of analysis rather than the organisation (although the latter is still important).

Operational implications

Providing technical support
In order to maximise a demand oriented community based approach, communities need a variety of types of support; information, guidance, organisational

support and capacity building. Technical support to communities should include items such as facilitating the organisation of community meetings, allowing communities to make their own decisions, deciding what they want to do about them, and explaining how proposed projects can be of help. The role for support agencies is one of explaining the range of technical options, the implications for each option, financial and other costs, and how decisions may affect the wider environment. Where locally provided facilities connect to wider city-wide facilities in vertically unbundled systems, there is a need to consider the arrangements for guaranteeing the linkages and assigning roles and responsibilities, both managerial and financial.

In many cases, government agencies may not be best placed to provide the type of support needed, or at the time it is needed, and these skills may be found in other intermediaries, most probably in NGO's or consultants. A key challenge for SSA is the need to understand what criteria can be used to determine if a particular intermediary is suitable for government and donors in providing technical support (Wright, 1997)

The shift in thinking away from the State as the sole provider of services and goods towards a role as enabling and facilitating other agencies to provide services and support is well documented. In this arrangement, certain organisations act as intermediaries or brokers between communities and local governments, often getting the process of development started, initiating dialogue between communities and local authorities and translating government policy to communities. In many cities, NGO's have successfully involved themselves in people's development processes and developed an expertise in this field (UNCHS/CityNet, 1997). Within the sphere of in-frastructure provision, Choguill (1997), for example, cites local and international NGO's playing a key role in assisting communities develop their basic services as one of the ten steps to sustainable urban infrastructure.

There are many examples from the literature of NGO's acting in an intermediary role, providing the types of technical support described in SSA. In the Gajapura Bosevana case study in Sri Lanka, Hewawasam et al (1997) describes the role that SEVANATHA took in enabling community mobilisation, '...*SEVANATHA was responsible for community mobilisation, planning and organising the community education and training programmes, finding funds for construction, providing technical advice for the community during construction work, and training..of community leaders on maintenance of community infrastructure.*' Wright (1997) cites two examples to further illustrate this point, the well

22

documented Orangi Pilot Project in Karachi Pakistan (where OPP has built capacity to the extent that local organisations are able to plan and finance their own latrines, house drains and shallow sewers), and the work of the Dominican Institute of Integral Development (IDDI) working in La Zurza settlement (which led to creation of a local CBO, SODIZUR, and a three stage programme to improve basic services and infrastructure). These examples demonstrate NGO's roles as intermediaries in the development process.

Of greater interest for the application of SSA are lessons which are learnt from this role. The impact on NGO's of their increasingly prominent role in the development process is explored by Bebbington & Mitlin (1996). Their research indicated NGO capacity building should be seen not only as a means to an end, but as a process. The implications of this for individual NGO's is a greater emphasis on a coherent institutional structure and operation. As NGO's adapt to their 'gap filling' role in taking over former State based activities, institutional coherence becomes critical since the demands of this role require new operational skills, and make it harder for the NGO structures and activities to continue to match its original mission statement.

In the Gomti River Pollution Control project at Lucknow, a multi-consultancy approach (including NGO's) was adopted for the delivery of project inputs. Although well intentioned, this strategy led to difficulties in that a hierarchy of partners was established in which NGO's did not feature prominently (Harvey, 1996). Two key lessons to emerge were to treat intermediaries such as NGO's and consultants as separate agencies, rather than similar organisation types with similar modes of operation, and to consider how 'guardian' consultants could help develop NGO inputs. However, it is not clear whether this arrangement would be acceptable to all stakeholders as it is likely to lead to increased project expense.

Some commentators argue against the received wisdom of NGO's as the natural partner to facilitate intermediary functions (Varley et al, 1996,). While it is true that NGO's are seen as being more responsive to locally expressed demand and more effective in encouraging participation, there are concerns arising from any support role they might provide. These include:

• The danger of creating parallel structures that ignore the legitimate role of the public sector;

• The fact that some NGO's may be a platform for elites and politicians which will reduce their effectiveness as an intermediary;

- NGO's do not have the resources to cover large urban areas, and even if this were to be the case, they lack the regulatory powers and quantity and range of resources which government possesses (UNCHS/CityNet, 1997);

- Some NGO's may not be the best placed organisations to help the urban poor articulate demand;

- NGO's absorb considerable management time in complex project management environments (Harvey, 1996).

There is also a need to develop a clearer understanding of the limits of the NGO's role. Can NGO's manage the provision of collector sewers and sewage treatment, for instance? Even if they can, are they the best placed to assume this role? The evidence of the Collaborative Katchi Abadi Improvement Program (CKAIP) in Hyderabad, Pakistan suggests that that the answer to both of these questions may be no.

In the same way that much of the existing literature recommends new working practices in local government, Varley et al argue that NGO's also need to be pragmatic in their partnerships, being open to working with government and avoiding a confrontational atmosphere that may discourage rather than enhance their participation in local decisions/programmes. In each particular case, NGO's should be included in the institutional analysis for the programme, and their relative merits and disadvantages assessed. Procedures for integrating technical support from other agencies need to be flexible and there needs to be commitment amongst donors and government agencies to work with NGO's. Many NGO's are sceptical about government while at the same time many government officials are suspicious of NGO's (UNCHS/CityNet, 1997). A trust building process is required in these collaborations. If this is absent, then the NGO may be forced into a service delivery rather than capacity building role. In this case, project priorities, and timing of implementation and procurement procedures may need to be changed to provide greater flexibility to allow NGO's to design and implement their own programmes.

Carrol et al (1995) provide a useful overview of the key criteria used to help determine whether a particular NGO is likely to be a suitable intermediary for governments and donors. Several indicators that an NGO meets the preconditions involved in effective partnerships include: flat management structures with decentralised authority; organisational structures at community level for decision making; use of iterative planning with local community; contributions of cash, labour or materials by local community; staff recruitment criteria, incentives and training that supports participation; positive perceptions of the NGO by local community leaders and turnover of client groups as they graduate over time.

However, in some cases, the qualities that make an NGO suitable as an intermediary may clash with government or donor requirements. In Zambia, the Squatter Upgrading Project agreed in principle to pursue long term community development goals by promoting active beneficiary participation. However, a key precondition was that if the collective self help approach was used by two intermediary NGO's and interfered with the project schedule, then contractors would be employed to complete the work rather than the NGO.

Key points:

- NGO's as intermediaries may be more flexible than the State, but they do not possess the same range of function or sphere of influence. Objective analyses of abilities and capacities are needed irrespective of organisation type;

- The changing role for NGO's in the development process may require them to adopt new institutional arrangements and modes of operation;

- Building partnerships with intermediaries requires flexibility in planning and implementation from local government;

- Technical know-how has to be transferred to the urban poor in an appropriate way. Simple, non-technical language that all will understand needs to be a requirement of any information sharing exercise.

Widening technological options

One of the lessons of the last two decades is that a lower cost technology is not in itself a guarantor of sustainable investments in sanitation services. Strategic sanitation's emphasis on demand requires consideration of not only lower cost technologies but a wider choice of technological options across the full cost range than was generally the case in the past.

A framework for analysing technological options is proposed which is based on a three way division of sanitation infrastructure levels: in-house, feeder and trunk. Levels of demand need to be assessed for each division (Wright, 1997).

A distinctive feature of demand oriented programmes is that users are allowed to make choices from a range (or 'menu') of sanitation options with appropriate price tags. However, there are few practical examples from the literature which exemplify this 'menu' approach to sanitation technologies. In many notable cases, including OPP, Bangladesh SIP, the Gajabapur-Bosevana settlement in Sri Lanka, and the Cuttack Urban Services Improvement Project it is clear that individual communities were not made aware of a range of technological options, their differing costs and suitability to specific areas. In effect, choices were made on behalf of the user community by sector professionals.

The idea of widening technological options as proposed through SSA raises a number of difficulties which can be addressed from two perspectives: the users' and service providers. Ideally, choice is based on an assessment of different options which is informed by timely and relevant information. It also assumes that the person making the choice understands the consequences (technical, managerial, financial) of that option. In practice, this is rarely the case, and choices are made on incomplete, or poorly informed knowledge. There is little discussion of this point when advocating the widening of technological options.

On one level, 'choice' for users may be limited because of the inadequacy of information about alternative options available at the local level. In this context, users may express a preference for systems which they see around them and which are familiar. However, this is not to be confused with the idea of choice based on a reasoned assessment of known alternatives. Furthermore, SSA fails to recognise the potential problem of partially informed user choices. Where community knowledge is based on an incomplete or inadequate understanding of the technical consequences of different systems in particular circumstances (i.e., choice of sewerage system in area without piped water supply), then there is a danger that user choices will affect system sustainability.

In contrast to these points, the experiences of NSDF/SPARC/MM in various Indian cities suggest otherwise, and Kurup (1997) argues that these programmes indicate that communities are capable of making technical decisions about

26

(and between) sanitation systems. Analysis of lessons learnt indicate the poor are capable of:

- Analysing their own settlement and sanitation needs;

- Planning, locating, designing and constructing community toilets;

- Partly paying for toilets and infrastructure improvements within settlements;

- Organising strategies for managing and maintaining these toilets

What is required is that the debate about technological options should not be overly rigid (Tayler, 1996). It is apparent that some community choices may have limitations which are obvious and serious; in other cases, it may be that the preferred options of both professionals and the people prove to have weaknesses. In these instances, a degree of negotiation takes place, *"...in which the sharing of views and information results in a third, more appropriate option being found "* (Tayler, 1996:12).

From the service providers perspective, one of the assumptions underpinning widening technological options is that engineers and other professionals are willing and able to adopt a wider range of sanitation options as 'appropriate'. In practice, this is not always the case. Didactic methods of education and university courses based on the problems of western industrialised countries tend to constrain innovative engineering approaches. The prevailing work culture within government or municipal sanitation departments acts against the adoption of 'alternative' engineering designs. Although most government service positions bring with them a high degree of employee security, many officers are unwilling to take professional risks and well established procedures are adhered to scrupulously (Evans, 1995). Although standard technology designs and use of technical manuals help to reduce design costs, they also stifle innovation. Standard designs are advocated not because they are necessarily the most appropriate solution, but because in the event of failure it is possible to shift blame onto the wider 'system'.

This point is reinforced in research examining the performance of on-plot sanitation in low income urban areas, where it is observed that, *"...[there is] an underlying feeling amongst some authorities and sector professionals that whilst on-plot sanitation was appropriate for rural areas, it was generally unsuitable in the urban context, unless viewed as a (preferably short term) route to 'better' forms of sanitation. All too often, assessments and judgements on the effectiveness and appropriateness [of plot systems] are made from a technologically biased and purely external perspective"* (Cotton and Saywell, 1998:3)

Irrespective of the user and service provider perspectives, in practice, choice is often constrained by a variety of factors, including technical, social, institutional and other issues (UNDP-World Bank Water and Sanitation Programme, 1996). Technical problems vary according to the system in question, but for sewerage may relate to flat topography and the lack of necessary gradients. Cotton (1998b) reinforces this point with lessons drawn from Cuttack, where user choice was limited because the topography of the city restricted horizontal unbundling of technologies. Other concerns include the integrity of materials and components used in sewered options, or the design standards for sewer diameters, gradients, and the siting of manholes and chambers. On plot systems present different technical issues, relating mainly to plot size, disposal of sullage water, impact of groundwater pollution from densely spaced pit latrines, operation of twin and double pit systems and desludging and disposal of latrines. Many of these issues are discussed in Cotton and Saywell (1998).

Institutional factors can limit choices when overly complex systems are advocated, and the technical capacity for O&M and management is lacking or cannot be sustained in the future. Cotton (1997) develops this point and questions the validity of conventional engineering planning and design which focuses on technical options and their technical feasibility as the primary determinants of success in implementation and sustainability. The requirements of a particular technical option ultimately need to fit with the local capacity that exists both within local government and local communities to cope with the infrastructure. Hence, the key factor in widening technological options needs to be a consideration of the technical, financial and managerial capacity to cope.

Key points:

- Widening sanitation options implies that choices between systems can be made. In practice there are many factors which constrain choice for users including lack of information, lack of appreciation of the impacts and consequences of different technical approaches and existence of subsidies for some technological options which skew choices;

- Sector professionals choices about sanitation for the urban poor tend to reflect prevailing (Western oriented) engineering solutions;

- The institutional set up within local government mitigates against innovation and 'alternative' technical approaches;

Key question:

- How can (reliable) comparisons between system performance be integrated into the planning process and made available to users in a form which is easily comprehensible?

Assessing sanitation demand

A demand oriented approach to sanitation is responsive, rather than prescriptive and one in which stakeholders are drawn into the process of decision making at all stages, including assessments of sanitation demand. Instead of governments or service utilities deciding which peri-urban communities should be provided with what type and level of service, the decisions are made jointly, through consultation and negotiations among all interested beneficiaries. All participants in a sanitation programme need to be aware of the implications of the options open to them, and it is the role of the implementing agency to explain technology options, costs, financing packages, and institutional arrangements involved in these options. Implementing agencies may set demand based eligibility criteria for sanitation interventions (i.e., community contributions to project costs, or O&M activities); alternatively, needs based criteria (i.e. health and poverty indicators) may be used to prioritise regions, but only for those who have expressed a willingness to pay (Wright, 1997).

Misjudgements about consumer demand are important contributing factors to poor sanitation system design and performance (World Bank, 1992). Demand assessment is critical therefore because it serves as a means by which system sustainability can be enhanced. It does this through facilitating decision-making, particularly on the quality of service and cost recovery policy which reflects what people want and are willing to pay.

SSA advocates willingness to pay surveys (WTP) as the main method to assess demand. Alternative approaches, such as affordability rule of thumb and benefit transfer have been found to lead to serious inaccuracies (DFID,

1997). For example, an affordability approach neglects research indicating that income is only one of several determinants of willingness to pay (Whittington et al, 1992). Differences in characteristics of supply, including cost, reliability and quality, between the improved and alternative sources of supply are also important, as are the socio-economic characteristics of the household and attitudes to government policy (World Bank Water Demand Research Team, 1993). In general, although these alternative approaches may give an indication of the current costs consumers bear for services, they fail to take account of the benefits from improved services, or how many households will use the improved system (Department for International Development (DFID), 1997).

The contingent valuation method (CVM), and its variants, have received much attention in the literature on demand assessment. In particular, Altaf and Hughes (1994) and Whittington (1998) have reviewed the use of CVM in measuring demand for services (in most cases relating to water supply) in developing countries. Several key advantages over other techniques can be identified; it can be used to study willingness to pay at different levels of service not currently available, it can help to determine the full range of benefits from service improvements, and can indicate how many households will switch to a new system.

But the constraints on the use of the technique are significant. Specialist expertise in the framing of CVM questionnaires, in result analysis and interpretation is generally required, thereby increasing its cost (a thorough CVM study is estimated to cost at least £100,000), and reduces the potential for community based involvement in its administration. There are also question marks about the reliability of the method, particularly relating to the hypothetical nature of questions asked, and the danger that information obtained through community meetings may be subject to 'mob' effects, leading to bias. Cotton (1998) argues that the emphasis on demand assessment fails to recognise the very different circumstances in which these techniques have been applied. CVM and pure demand based approaches work well in the context of water supply schemes, deciding on standposts, yard connections and house connections, but these same techniques do not apply with the same clarity to sanitation projects. For example, in cases where only a few households receive a latrine on a demand led basis, the benefits of such service improvement are minimal if the households' neighbours are defecating in the open and contaminating the local environment. There are also unresolved issues relating to how demand is negotiated after it is expressed; what if some members of the community choose sewerage and others latrine based systems? How should the technical considerations inherent in these choices be integrated into community based expression of demand?

In order for demand assessment studies to realise their full potential (i.e., to inform policy choices at the strategic framework level, and to help shape the design of individual projects) it is essential that they are used at more than one stage in the project development process, and that they are integrated in such a way that their findings influence design choices (DFID, 1997). It is also observed that demand driven planning processes pose considerable implications for consultants, planners, economists and government officials, in that it requires them to be more flexible in their responses to user communities (Whittington et al, 1996). Consultants need to be willing to adopt an open minded approach to problems of basic service delivery, and consider different service scenarios for a community, based in part on the community's own desires. This is difficult in that there are few incentives for consultants to work in this way.

A central weakness of the emphasis placed on the need for demand driven approaches is the significant institutional change they imply, and the ability of those institutions to respond to a changed institutional culture. Demand driven approaches involve different processes than the formal supply driven process of urbanisation (WASH, 1993). Typically, urban sector institutions in developing countries are set up for the latter, and are not organisationally structured and prepared to carry out demand driven urbanisation. Institutions have their own laws and regulations, institution mission statements, goals, personnel and methods. Staff are trained in a supply oriented manner in their approach to urban planning, thus discussions of demand driven approaches often lead to confusion for staff about institutional and personal responsibilities towards peri-urban communities. An additional problem with the approach is that assessing demand becomes an exercise which can inflate expectations about service delivery, which could be years in delivering, or simply not feasible. Regardless of this, recent research suggests that moves towards participation and a 'demand' based approach are only likely to work if providers see ways in which these moves will help them to achieve their perceived objectives. (GHK R&T 1998).

A key element missing from SSA is recognition that demand for sanitation is more than a one-dimensional concept. RWSG - South Asia (1997) describe two levels of the concept, beginning with unexpressed or latent demand.

31

Although some projects, such as the Bangladesh Slum Improvement Project (SIP) may appear to be essentially supply driven, the fact that there was no formal assessment of sanitation demand does not imply that there was no demand for sanitation services. Demand may be present but remain unexpressed or latent. A key question then becomes how this latent demand can become explicit. A second division focuses on uninformed and informed demand. In the Orangi Pilot Project, Pakistan there was a clear expression of community demand for a solution to sanitation and drainage problems, but little consideration of concern for the wider environment. Discharge from Orangi's sewers flowed into open nullahs and polluted the Lyari river. Community demand, although explicit, was partially informed in that it failed to appreciate the impact on the downstream environment. Similarly, demand may be uninformed in cases where there is no consideration of the true financial and economic costs of an option, or possible technical difficulties associated with implementing particular sanitation options.

A related point is that demand is often based on what people know or see around them. How then is it possible for the community to demand options which they are unfamiliar with? Demand for a product, good or service does not occur in a vacuum; it is affected by the local context. Thus, RWSG-SA argue that there can never be a purely demand driven approach in the choice of technology because this must be influenced by the availability and cost, which are both supply side factors. For example, in Orangi, the choice of sewers was affected by the topography of the area which allowed gravity discharge to nullahs.

Key points:

- Demand and demand assessment are complex, multi-faceted issues. It is important to recognise different levels of demand, including latent or unexpressed and partially informed demand;

- There are many methods by which demand can be assessed, each with their own weaknesses. CVM is widely heralded in the sector, but question marks over reliability of results and the cost of the method remain;

- The demand driven approach brings with it new working requirements, such as an emphasis on participatory approaches and negotiating compromises with user groups that do not normally interact in traditional planning processes;

- The provision of services should be demand driven to the greatest extent possible but the choice of the way those services are provided must take account of supply side factors;

Key questions:

- How can reliability in demand assessment exercises be improved?

- Do formal sector institutions possess the skills, experience and institutional commitment necessary to change their approach to peri-urban communities?

Unbundling sanitation investments
'Unbundling' as a concept is a way of dividing investments into more realistic and manageable components, allowing for more appropriate and efficient use of resources.

SSA describes two types of unbundling. Horizontal unbundling involves the subdivision of services/technologies geographically, so that a city may be broken down into two or more zones, each with self contained and independent sanitation services. Dividing sanitation systems into zones helps to reduce the average diameters and depths of sewers when compared with a single centralised system, and as these are likely to be the two highest cost elements, it is probable that horizontal unbundling is sound economically wherever it is technically feasible. Unbundled systems may also be linked, for example at a treatment works or long outfall. An example of horizontal unbundling quoted by Wright is the case study of Manila, the Philippines, where the metropolitan area has been horizontally unbundled into two parts for the supply of water and sewerage services.

Secondly, there is vertical unbundling, where sanitation programmes are divided according to the scale and cost of the components. Division may apply to the design and construction phases, and to the O&M of the systems. Further subdividing is possible to permit community managed schemes to connect into publicly or privately operated sewerage systems. The key advantages of vertical unbundling are that it may provide flexibility in the financing of urban sanitation, and help to make connections affordable through equitable cross subsidy. It is particularly valuable in that it helps to separate investment decisions on in-house, feeder and trunk levels thereby allowing a clear link to be made between benefits and costs. The condominial sewerage systems of Brazil are cited as an example of this form of unbundling.

Unbundling as a whole may lead to progress on the development of city wide sanitation programmes that would have stalled if financed and implemented as a single package (Wright, 1997).

In sanitation programmes, unbundling is a new term which to an extent describes established practices. Horizontal unbundling typically takes place when different technological options are used in separate parts of a city, such as when on-plot systems are used in some districts, and conventional water borne sewerage in others. Likewise, vertical unbundling can be found in many sanitation systems in that services within the plot boundary are normally the householders' responsibility, while those beyond the plot are in the public domain and provided by local authorities or government.

In the proceedings for a regional workshop on sanitation for low income urban communities, RWSG - South Asia (1997) make two general observations about the unbundling concept. The first reinforces the idea that unbundling is not a new concept; what is new is the manner in which it is described. Clear similarities exist between unbundling and the idea of 'moving the boundary' between private/community sector provision. It has become accepted practice in development that it is best to leave responsibility for facilities and services within the plot to householders, with a support service role being fulfilled by the public sector. 'Moving the boundary' recognises that local stakeholders are well placed to undertake the roles of provision and management of some services beyond this traditional plot boundary division. In consequence, the public sector's role is shifted towards the connections between secondary and tertiary facilities. Parallels between this shifting of responsibilities and the idea of disaggregating roles through an unbundled approach are clear.

Secondly, RWSG - South Asia observe that with the unbundling of responsibilities there is greater scope for independent activity at the local level than is generally the case with higher order facilities. This is illustrated through the example of a hypothetical sewerage scheme: provision of sewers at the local level will be dependent on the presence of suitable secondary sewers for receipt of discharge. Hence the need for an integrated approach. However, tertiary sewers can be provided independently in streets and lanes once secondary sewers and appropriate disposal facilities have been constructed. The critical point is that the closer to the household level, the greater the scope for horizontal unbundling to take place.

Horizontal unbundling is possible when part of a sanitation system is managed independently of other facilities at the same level. RWSG - South Asia (1997) cite two examples of projects in which such unbundling has occurred: Sukkur, India, and Sri Lanka. In each case, faecal waste and sullage from each district are handled separately from sanitation networks in adjacent urban areas. For example, in the Sri Lankan example, sewers discharge to the settlement-level septic tanks. Additionally, the OPP experience in Pakistan reinforces the opportunities for horizontal unbundling at the lower or local end of vertically integrated systems, despite centralised control over higher order facilities. In this project, horizontal unbundling was observed at lane level, with individual lane organisations drawing up different strategies to manage the sewerage system (Siddiqui and Rashid, 1997).

Vertical unbundling is to some extent inherent in all sanitation systems in which a hierarchical system exists in which facilities and services are provided at a number of levels. This hierarchy is most explicity seen in a sewered system where on-plot facilities are connected to branch sewers which are connected to collector and trunk sewers which direct sewage to some form of treatment before being discharged into the wider environment. Wright argues for a three level distinction of facilities, in-house, feeder and trunk levels. OPP differentiate a four level typology including in-house (on-plot), local feeder, secondary feeder/collector and primary/city wide facilities. The latter definition has the advantage of distinguishing between tertiary level facilities that would appear to present opportunities for community action and secondary level facilities which would appear to be best provided by central authorities.

The Bangladesh SIP illustrates vertical unbundling on two levels. Initially, the project separated responsibilities between a project management unit (responsible for services within the project) and government agencies which continued to deliver services to the city as a whole. Furthermore, within the project management unit there existed a four tier structure (including women's groups, sub-project implementation committee, project implementation committee and central co-ordination committee), which attempted to further unbundle responsibilities between these particular sections.

Further lessons from vertical unbundling can be found from OPP, where it was found that the effectiveness of devolving responsibility for finance, management and maintenance of the sanitation system depends critically on institutionalising community mobilisation and training procedures and on the degree of transparency in working with government agencies (Siddiqui and Rashid, 1997).

The collection of excreta from large numbers of on-plot sanitation systems is a sanitation activity which can be organised in such a way as to allow for unbundling of responsibilities (Muller, 1997). In an analysis of four case studies from Ghana, Tanzania, India and China, a wide variety of actors were found to be employed in the collection process, including informal, small scale enterprises, local scavengers, formal private enterprises and even municipal labourers. The process involves four stages: removal/primary transfer to neighbourhood collection point; secondary transfer; treatment and disposal. In general, the role of private formal/informal organisation tends to concentrate on the removal/primary transfer stage of the process, with secondary transfer, treatment and disposal predominantly the responsibility of municipal departments, although in Tanzania, large scale informal waste collectors were involved in treatment. As with other experiences of unbundled systems, Muller stresses the need for linkages between the separate parts, arguing that, *"...primary collection must be linked to a larger sanitation system that operates facilities for treatment and disposal of excreta "* (Muller, 1997:71). The internal functioning of municipal sanitation departments, their capacity to manage personnel, equipment and finance is viewed as a key element in influencing its ability to interact with other organisations in the process.

The potential benefit of unbundling responsibilities is demonstrated in a case study of innovative approaches to solid waste management in three Bangladeshi municipalities (Gaffar and Rahman, 1997). In this case, the solid waste chain was unbundled according to physical handling responsibilities, and the key outcomes recorded were a 20-25 per cent reduction in budget costs during the two year operation of the project, an improvement in service provision for householders (drains were cleared, waste was removed from streets), and positive reactions to the project from users.

Although these case studies demonstrate the way in which either horizontal or vertical unbundling has been achieved, the literature review provides several examples of risks associated with unbundling. Matin (1997) when commenting on the Bangladesh SIP argues that vertical unbundling had mixed results in this project, primarily because the management structure meant planning decisions tended to be dominated at the programme implementation committee and central co-ordination committee level. Community level groups, such as women's groups and sub-project implementation committee tended to implement what had been decided at higher levels.

One of the weaknesses from unbundling is that little attention is paid to how links are made between disaggregated systems. Cotton (1998b) cites experiences from the Department for International Development (DFID) sponsored Cuttack Urban Services Improvement Project (CUSIP) which illustrate this point. The three key agencies with a stake in urban sanitation in Cuttack include the CUSIP, Cuttack Municipal Corporation (CkMC) and the Public Health Engineering Department (PHED). Each agency has adopted different programmes for sanitation, and these are unbundled to the extent that there are different institutional responsibilities and financing arrangements for on-plot, neighbourhood and centralised infrastructure. The key problem for Cuttack, and a lesson for SSA as a whole, is that unbundling can only take place in the context of a strategic framework, where there is some provision for co-ordination of activities. Rather than arguing for further unbundling, there is a need for 'bundling up' in some cases, to ensure that the each agency is aware of each others' roles and responsibilities. An additional concern raised from this point is that of the institutional capacity required to deal with unbundling, and resolution of questions such as who oversees the process and who co-ordinates the constituent parts.

Tayler (1997b) cites experiences of sewerage systems in Pakistan that have been unbundled with responsibilities shared between agencies, leading to sustainability problems with the systems. In Northeast Lahore, the design of tertiary and some secondary sewers was the responsibility of the upgrading unit in the Metropolitan Planning Wing of the Lahore Development Authority, whilst ongoing O&M was assigned to Lahore Water and Sanitation Agency (WASA). Two problems arose from this division of responsibility: WASA's failure to complete construction of off-site sewers and a reluctance to accept 'appropriate' design standards advocated by the designers. Hasan (1997) reports a similar problem in Sukkur, where a PHED designed main trunk sewer had been inoperable for 15 years, due to partial sewer collapse and the failure of pumping stations. Although PHED received funds for new works, no provision was made for repair and O&M from Sukkur Municipal Corporation. This may be because no formal arrangement was made between key stakeholders regarding financing of the project running costs. Hasan comments that collaboration between SMC-PHED could have been achieved when the funding allocations were being made by the provincial government. However, no such co-ordination was present.

Both the Bangladesh SIP and the OPP projects have experienced problems with linking aspects of their unbundled systems. In Bangladesh, SIP drains and the city wide drainage systems do not coincide, leaving SIP drains discharging pools of polluted water on the periphery of the slums (RWSG - South Asia (1997)). Similarly, there has been little progress to date on provision of trunk sewerage in Orangi.

Key points:

- Unbundling of technologies and responsibilities is not always possible or desirable. In some cases, re-bundling to ensure that disaggregated systems coincide, or improved co-ordination of sector agencies, is required;

- The Bangladesh SIP and Pakistan OPP projects point to the need for integration of local level plans into city wide infrastructure;

- There are parallels between the concepts of unbundling and 'moving the boundary' between private /community sector provision and co-production of services;

- The interface between local authorities (formal/complex) and communities (informal) has a key impact on the success of unbundling responsibilities;

- " *Unbundling of systems implies a need for a range of standards to suit different levels* " (UNDP-World Bank Water and Sanitation Group RWSG - South Asia, 1997:14)

Financing and cost recovery

SSA argues for a central role to be given to user charges with regard to financing. This means that users are encouraged to contribute according to their willingness and ability to pay for the services they have chosen as best meeting their needs. The rationale for this approach is based on the lessons learnt from previous city wide, donor financed projects. Typically, these schemes were dependent on widespread subsidies to get projects off the ground because it was assumed that users did not have adequate means to pay. The consequence was unsustainable interventions.

The demand based approach to SSA provides a way to think through how the costs of sanitation can be best shared, and it also provides reliable information on the value that users place on sanitation improvements and on their WTP for those benefits. Wright advocates a model of financing sanitation improvement which is based on appropriate cost recovery at household, block, neighbourhood, city and river basin level.

Direct user payments: User WTP is generally limited to those benefits that users perceive and are able to internalise. User WTP may be insufficient to pay for the full cost of systems, including trunk sewers and treatment, thus, some form of complementary finance will be required. The examples of OPP and PROSANEAR show that user WTP should be tested before considering cross subsidies from other user groups or external provision of funds. Not all direct user payments need to be in cash, but in-kind contributions have to be voluntary and must tangibly reduce the real financial cost of providing the service. Household borrowing to finance user payment is acceptable - the most effective system for ensuring user payment for sanitation have been those insisting on front end payments for construction and access to the service. Examples of credit systems are known, including Lesotho's low cost urban sanitation scheme.

Collective payments from block and neighbourhoods: Neighbourhood groups may be useful in organising collective payments (although there may be problems in group decision making). In OPP, neighbourhood groups helped provide finance for neighbourhood collection systems. In both OPP and PROSANEAR, groups were able to encourage individuals to sign on to less costly neighbourhood schemes, and to undertake the O&M for them, than the existing sanitation organisations had been able to do. Neighbourhood groups were instrumental in convincing technical staff that cheaper options could work well, at costs that households could afford.

Collective payments from local and national governments: Directly or indirectly government participates in the financing of sanitation services in all countries (i.e. financial support to users, allocation of funds for investments, taxes and control of credit allocations).

39

The financial premise of SSA is to base financial requirements on what is worthwhile to finance, rather than assuming that if something can be financed, it is worthwhile. Government finance has been extensively used in the past as a substitute for user charges and has benefited those who already have access to services, rather than compensating service providers for external benefits of extending services to users who are not willing or able to pay. One outcome of this is a continuing reluctance to extend service coverage to the poor; also relatively little expansion of treatment facilities to protect water sources and insufficient maintenance of existing facilities for those with connections (Wright, 1997).

The shift in development thinking away from supply-led financing strategies to those that are demand-based implies that if the financial element of a sanitation programme is to be sustainable, then considerable information about the financial context in which communities operate will be required. This includes, *"...information relating to the availability of credit facilities, the willingness of the communities to pay for sanitation, government attitudes towards cost recovery, the role of the private sector and so on "*. (Cotton and Saywell, 1998:35) SSA's premise on financing and cost recovery is that sound finances are best achieved where costs are borne either directly or indirectly by the users of sanitation services.

OPP illustrates one aspect of this point, relating to capital costs, with the users of tertiary sewers in Orangi managing their construction and paying their full cost, without subsidy or loan arrangement. Construction costs for lane level and secondary sewage lines in Orangi were approximately Rs. 1000, collected through lane level organisations charged with the responsibility. This method of cost recovery has an additional benefit of offering transparency /accountability of financing arrangements at the local level. (Siddiqui and Rashid, 1997). A variation on the Orangi approach is that adopted in the Faisalabad Area Upgrading Project (FAUP), where tertiary level sewers were paid through equal contributions from users and government inputs to the FAUP (UNDP-World Bank Water and Sanitation Group RWSG - South Asia (1996)). In neither case was any attempt made to recover the capital costs of higher-order facilities directly. Thus, the overall levels of cost recovery are rather lower than those suggested above.

Many sanitation projects attempt to recover costs from users. However, approaches vary considerably, and the effectiveness of recovery schemes may be adversely affected by the local operational context. NSDF/SPARC/

MM found in Dharavi, Bombay that it was difficult to implement effective cost recovery schemes in situations where users had become used to receiving services free of charge (UNDP-World Bank Water and Sanitation Group RWSG - South Asia, 1997). Additionally, there are problems associated with cost recovery schemes which operate alongside projects where no attempt at cost recovery is made.

SSA argues that borrowing to finance direct user payment is acceptable, although relatively little attention is paid to the use of credit mechanisms, beyond citing the Lesotho sanitation scheme. Cost recovery in sanitation projects is achievable, and credit schemes offer a system for attaining this goal. Varley (1997) cites several lessons learnt from household credit financing schemes for sanitation, including:

- The costs involved in financing credit schemes can be lowered where borrowers use existing informal financial intermediaries rather than developing new collection systems;

- It may be easier to arrange cost recovery when sanitation is combined with other community development activities;

- Expansion of coverage must be balanced with resources spent on recovery of loans and relending money to new borrowers;

- An incremental approach to lending allows the borrower to gradually increase debt burden, and the lender to assess credit-worthiness or debt capacity.

Additionally, Cotton and Saywell (1998) abstract key lessons learnt from a variety of cost recovery schemes relating to the provision of household level sanitation facilities:

- Use of social rather than legal sanctions to enforce recovery;

- The need for transparency in repayment arrangements - householders must have access to and understand the status of recovery systems;

- Repayment schedules need to recognise and accommodate periods of financial stress for the householder;

- Interviewing potential beneficiaries before granting loans may help to reduce defaulting. In Ouagadougou, Burkina Faso, users under the

Strategic Sanitation Plan were filtered according to their ability to make substantial savings (Saidi-Sharouze, 1994).

Although OPP and FAUP demonstrate that direct cost recovery of capital costs through user contributions is possible, there are still questions relating to community preparedness to pay for on-going running costs of the systems. In OPP it was evident that many users were unwilling to assume the necessary responsibility for financing recurrent costs of maintenance given the frequency with which the systems had to be cleaned and the rising charges made by scavengers for this maintenance service. In consequence, it was found that regular cleaning of manholes, pipes and replacement of covers was often left unattended. It may be that this situation reflects general technical problems with sewers in low-income areas where silt loads are high and poor solid waste collection systems increase the likelihood that solids will enter the sewer. These technical problems impose unacceptably high maintenance costs that users are eventually unwilling to meet. (Tayler, 1997b).

On a more general level, the debate surrounding the financing of urban services is addressed specifically by Rondinelli (1990). The transfer of administrative and financial responsibilities for urban services to municipalities is seen as one way in which increasing demands on services can be met, at the same time as relieving some of the fiscal pressure on central treasuries. However, decentralisation alone is not a panacea for financial problems. In particular, central government will be unable to decentralise without first strengthening municipal administrative capacity, and addressing the problems of poor organisational structures and operating procedures.

Key points:

- In demand led projects, financing for sanitation facilities requires considerable information about the financial environment of communities;

- It may be difficult to achieve cost recovery in cases where users have become used to receiving services free of charge;

- Credit mechanisms are increasingly used to finance sanitation projects; many useful and valuable lessons have been abstracted from these case studies (i.e. use of informal financial intermediaries; combining sanitation with other aspects of community development);

- Some case studies indicate difficulty over community prepared-ness to pay for on-going maintenance costs of sanitation systems.

Key questions:

- Are stakeholders with a limited financial stake in the provision of facilities willing to finance the ongoing O&M of those facilities?

- There are issues of equity associated with the financing and cost recovery aspects of SSA: should the urban poor pay when richer communities don't?

Miscellaneous issues
Small steps approach
The small steps approach in relation to SSA implies a recognition of the links between physical infrastructure provision and the existing institutional/ financial capacity to cope with such activities. It also allows for lessons learnt from experience to be reinvested into the on-going planning process. Such an approach is seen as fundamental if sanitation provision is to be a shared process of learning rather than the application of discrete solutions.

Relatively few sources in the literature explicitly discuss this matter. UNDP-World Bank Water and Sanitation Group RWSG - South Asia (1997) is one exception to this rule, citing case studies where such an approach has been tried:

- In India, the Dharavi and P.D' Melo Road cases show how mistakes were incorporated into the planning and design of later projects;

- The Siddharthapura project in Sri Lanka exemplifies the adoption of an incremental approach to the upgrading of service levels;

- OPP in Karachi, Pakistan shows how initial activities in one small part of Orangi turned into a programme that covered all its area and then expanded to other projects and cities in Pakistan.

All these initiatives dealt with either local, relatively self-contained facilities or the local components of vertically unbundled systems. In some cases, such facilities have proved impossible to operate effectively in the absence of higher-order facilities which often have to be provided in larger steps. It would appear that the small-steps approach will often require judgement and it is arguable that the emphasis should be on appropriate steps, kept as small as possible, rather than small steps per-se.

Key point:
- The small steps approach will only function when appropriate facilities are available at the larger (district/city wide) scale;

Key question:
- How can large and small investments be incorporated into planning a programme which is flexible enough to cope with the separate demands of planning on multi-levels and which still takes account of demand expressed by users?

Strategies of institutional design: broadening competition
One of the assumptions underpinning SSA is that broadening competition is a mechanism by which operational efficiency can be achieved with minimal transaction costs.

Recent research findings question this assumption. Batley (1996) investigated the extent to which private sector involvement led to improved delivery of a range of urban services (although admittedly not sanitation) in six developing countries. The study made comparisons of the ways in which local level services were provided in cities in Brazil, Mexico, Uganda, Zimbabwe, India and Malaysia. Although in some cases there was evidence to suggest better private performance in service delivery, it was not possible to conclude that privatisation automatically led to greater efficiency and effectiveness overall. Key points arising from the research with relevance to SSA include:

- The 'better' performance of private entrepreneurs was in part due to the fact that they managed easier sectors of the market.

- In those cases where there was no private competition, a fully public service performed in many instances as well as a public-private partnership arrangement in other countries.

- There are advantages from forms of private participation in service delivery (including consumer orientation, decentralised management and civil control of bureaucracy).

In practice it may be difficult for weak public administrations to undertake new roles which follow from partial privatisations, such as setting policy frameworks, managing contracts, regulating contractors and financing/ supporting producers and consumers.

Part C: Conclusions

What is it that is new about the strategic sanitation approach? Wright argues that its *distinctive* features are its emphasis on stakeholder participation and an incentive driven approach. But this should not be confused for innovation or novelty, since it would be difficult to claim that SSA's emphasis on participatory processes, demand orientation, or the need for adequate motivation amongst sector agencies are new ideas for the experienced sector professional. There are also conceptual parallels between SSA and other approaches to urban planning, including Multi-Sector Investment Planning (MSIP) and Integrated Urban Infrastructure Development (IUID). However, it is possible to identify ideas about the approach which distinguish it from other attempts at organising the provision of urban sanitation and these include:

- The attempt that SSA makes at integrating a wide spectrum of factors impacting on sanitation into a framework that organises and guides planning;

- The recognition of a 'political' dimension to sanitation planning, as described in sections relating to perverse incentives;

The following key points emerged from the literature review:

- Few, if any, projects can claim to have adopted all or the majority of SSA concepts into project design and management. Many of the case studies which are cited in this review comment on aspects of SSA which have been identified in projects conceived without knowledge of the conceptual framework. Only two case studies (Kumasi SSP and Ouagadougou SSO) have explicitly applied SSA principles. In many instances, the review indicates that further work is required to demonstrate that SSA is a tool which can be applied in its entirety.

- One of the key weaknesses of the SSA is the lack of practical guidance on how to initiate, design and implement sanitation interventions using its key concepts. In part, that is the responsibility of the pilot planning phase of DFID funded project R6875 (Practical Development of Strategic

47

Sanitation Concepts). However, Howard (1996, 1997) provides a first step in addressing this gap through the description of a diagnostic study approach and analysis of the methodology involved in such a task. Strategic development of sanitation service provision in urban areas depends on a thorough understanding of all the key issues and problems which affect the sector and its performance. National diagnostic studies provide the situational analysis required to assess strengths and weaknesses and to highlight key areas for attention. Good data collection, identification of key principles, and the linking of sector assessments with policy development are key lessons learnt from the application of this approach in Zambia.

- A critical issue focuses on the kind of skills needed to initiate sanitation interventions in peri-urban communities using SSA. Formal institutions must be prepared to move away from standard technology and approaches (which are often inappropriate) and move towards creative solutions and alternative technologies. Engineers and planners in formal institutions must be able and willing to identify and work with existing community representatives.

- Stakeholder participation is not automatic. Incentives, targeted at differing groups, need to be established early in project design and management. Particular attention has to be paid to the way in which different stakeholders interact in the provision of infrastructure.

- Incentives for participation are context specific and are not necessarily replicable to other projects. Perverse incentives need to be tackled on two fronts: addressing the reasons why they arise and how they are sustained. Corrective action is best focused through individuals rather than at the institutional level.

- NGO's can and do act as intermediaries to provide a wide range of support services for infrastructure provision. However, the limitations, as well as the advantages of using NGO's to provide support needs to be fully recognised.

- SSA implies new ways of working for stakeholders. The difficulties of adapting to changed circumstances, roles, responsibilities are not widely reported or acknowledged. The capacity to adapt to new arrangements is critical to the success of the approach.

- The notion of widening sanitation options sounds an attractive concept, but is difficult and complex to achieve, depending as it does on concepts of choice. The exercise of choice can be constrained by poor or inadequate information at the local level, and by the entrenched vested interests of service providers.

- Unbundling is a new term which describes established practice. Unbundling is not applicable in all situations; in fact, many projects suffer from excessive disaggregation of responsibilities and technologies, leading to problems of agency co-ordination and sanitation systems which fail to link up. The point at which formal and informal communities interact is a key aspect of the success of unbundled systems.

References

ABBOT, J. (1996) *Sharing the City: Community participation in urban management*. Earthscan Publications. London, UK

ALTAF, A. and HUGHES, J.A. (1994) 'Measuring the Demand for Improved Sanitation Services: Contingent Valuation Study in Ouagadougou, Burkina Faso'. *Urban Studies*, Vol. 31, **10**, pp 1763-1776

BATLEY, R.A. (1996) 'Public-Private Relationships and Performance in Service Provision'. *Urban Studies*, Vol. 33, **4-5**, pp 723-751

BEBBINGTON, A., and MITLIN, D. (1996) NGO Capacity and Capacity Building: Summary of Report to ESCOR. International Institute for Environment and Development (IIED), London.

CARROL, T., SCHMIDT, M., and BEBBINGTON, T. (1995) 'Participation and Intermediary NGO's' The World Bank, *Environment Department Dissemination Notes*, Number 22, The World Bank, Washington D.C., USA

CHOGUILL, C. (1997) 'Ten Steps to Sustainable Urban Infrastructure'. *Urban Age* Vol. 5, **2**, pp 22-23

COTTON, A.P. (1997) Sanitation Options - India. WELL Task No. 18 Water and Environmental Health, London and Loughborough (WELL), Loughborough University, UK.

COTTON, A.P. (1998), (Director of Urban Programmes, Loughborough University, UK), Personal communication.

COTTON, A.P. (1998b) Discussion Paper on SSA Implications in Cuttack, India. Unpublished report, WEDC, Loughborough University, UK.

COTTON, A.P., FRANCEYS, R.W., PICKFORD, J.A., and SAYWELL, D.L. (1995) *On Plot Sanitation in Low Income Urban Communities: A Review of Literature* WEDC, Loughborough University, UK.

COTTON, A.P. and SAYWELL, D.L. (1998) *On Plot Sanitation in Low Income Urban Communities: Guidelines for selection*. WEDC, Loughborough University, UK

DAVIDSON, F. (1996) 'Planning for Performance: Requirements for sustainable development'. *Habitat International*, Vol. 20, **3**, pp 445-462

DELHI ACTION GROUP and MAHILA HOUSING TRUST (1997) Lessons Learned: Urban Partnerships in Ahmedabad Presentation document

DEPARTMENT FOR INTERNATIONAL DEVELOPMENT (1997) Demand Assessment in the Water and Sanitation Sector: Reflections on a DFID Seminar. Report from a seminar held in London, December 1997

DESAI, V. (1996) Access to power and participation, *TWPR*, 18 **(2)**

EHP (1997) Activity report No. 34: Designing a Sanitation Programme for the Urban Poor: Case Study from Montego Bay, Jamaica. Environmental Health Project, US Agency for International Development, Washington DC, USA

ENCHEVERRI-GENT (1992) 'Public Participation and Poverty Alleviation: The Experience of Reform Communists in India's West Bengal'. *World Development*, 20, **10**: 1401-22

EVANS, B. (1995) *Institutional Incentives and the Provision of Urban Sanitation: Can the Community Increase the Chances of Success*? Essay submitted in partial fulfilment of an MSc degree in the Faculty of Economics (Development Studies). London School of Economics and Political Science.

FOUNDATION FOR PUBLIC INTEREST (1997) Performance Review Rating: Urban Management Tool. Report Card of Poor Self-employed Women on Public Services in Ahmedabad. Presentation by Mihir Bhatt at City Leaders and Municipal Officials of Gujarat, May 6 & 7, 1997 Foundation for Public Interest, Ahmedabad

GAFFAR, A. and RAHMAN, M. (1997) Unbundling of Responsibilities: Roles of Different Organisations in the Sector. Paper No.2, National Workshop on Strategic Sanitation Approach, LGED, Bangladesh

GHK RESEARCH AND TRAINING (1998) Case studies and Draft Final Report, ENGKARS project R6862 Building Municipal Capacity for Community Participation

HARVEY, M. (1996) Gomti River Pollution Control Project at Lucknow - Phase 1. Lessons identified: handover notes, December 1996. Unpublished document.

HARVEY, M.(1998), (Engineering Field Manager, Department for International Development), Personal communication.

HASAN, A (1992) Manual for Rehabilitation Programmes for Informal Settlements based on Orangi Pilot Project Model, OPP-RTI, Karachi.

HASAN, A. (1997) *Working with Government: The story of OPP's collaboration with state agencies for replicating its low cost sanitation programme.* City Press, Karachi, Pakistan.

HEWAWASAM, H.T., PATHIRAGE, D., and JAYARATNE, K.A., (1997) Sanitation for Low Income Settlements: Evolving Strategic Approaches in Sri Lanka. Case study prepared for the UNDP-World Bank Water and Sanitation Programme Regional Workshop on Sanitation for Low Income Communities, February 23-25, 1997

HOWARD, G. (1996) *Urbanisation, Sanitation and Environmental Health.* Commonwealth Secretariat and Robens Institute, University of Surrey.

HOWARD, G. (1997) 'Strategic approaches to urban sanitation', in Pickford et al (Eds.) *Water and sanitation for all: partnerships and innovations. Proceedings from the 23rd WEDC Conference held in Durban, South Africa.* WEDC, Loughborough University, UK.

HUMAN SETTLEMENT MANAGEMENT INSTITUTE (1995) International Seminar: Integrated Urban Infrastructure Development. Human Settlement Management Institute, 212 Asian Games Village, New Delhi - 110049, India.

KURUP, B. (1997) Strategic Approaches to Sanitation: Experiences of NSDF, SPARC and Mahila Milan in Indian Cities - A Case Study. Prepared for the UNDP-World Bank Water and Sanitation Programme Regional Workshop on Sanitation for Low Income Communities, February 23-25, 1997

VAN DER LINDEN, J (1997) On popular participation in a culture of patronage; patrons and grassroots organisation in a sites and services project in Hyderabad, Pakistan, *Environment and Urbanisation*, 9 (**1**)

MAHILA HOUSING TRUST (1997) City-Women Partnerships in Ahmedabad: Lessons Learnt. Presentation to Delhi Action Group, September 1997

MANIKUTTY, S. (1997) 'Community participation: So What? Evidence From a Comparative Study of Two Rural Water Supply and Sanitation Projects in India'. *Development Policy Review*, Vol. 15, pp 1-26

MATIN, NILAFUR (1997) Community Participation and Sustainability: A Strategic Approach to Slum Improvement in Bangladesh. Prepared for the UNDP-World Bank Water and Sanitation Programme Regional Workshop on Sanitation for Low Income Communities, February 23-25, 1997

MEHTA, M. (1993) Convergence in UBSP: An Exploratory Study of Nasik and Aligarh. UNICEF, New Delhi, India

MULLER, M.S. (1997) (Ed.)*The Collection of Household Excreta: The operation of services in urban low income neighbourhoods*. Pathumthani: ENSIC/AIT. Urban Waste Series: 6, pp 73

PAUL, S. (1996) 'Report Cards: A Novel Approach for Improving Urban Services'. *The Urban Age*, January 1996, pp 7-16

PLUMMER, J. (1998) 'Capacity Building at Municipal Level'. *Urbanisation*, **6**, pp 4-5

RONDINELLI, D.A. (1990) 'Financing the Decentralisation of Urban Services in Developing Countries: Administrative Requirements for Fiscal Improvements'. *Studies in Comparative International Development*, 25, **2**, pp 43-59

RWSG - South Asia (1996) Improving Sanitation in Peri-urban Areas: Towards an Incentive-demand Approach. Draft section on urban sanitation for programme proposals, 24 April, 1996 Unpublished report

SAIDI-SHAROUZE, M. (1994) *Ouagadougou and Kumasi Sanitation Projects: A comparative case study*. UNDP-World Bank Water and Sanitation Programme RWSG-WA

SIDDIQUI, T., AND RASHID, A. (1997) Case Study of the Orangi Pilot Project Low Cost Sanitation Model. Prepared for the UNDP-World Bank Water and Sanitation Programme Regional Workshop on Sanitation for Low Income Communities, February 23-25, 1997

STEINBERG, F. (1996) 'Can Development Communication Improve Urban Management?' *Habitat International*, Vol. 20, **4**, pp 567-581.

TAYLER, K. (1996) *'Background issues paper'*, in UNDP-World Bank Water and Sanitation Group RWSG - South Asia (1996) *Proceedings of workshop on sanitation for poor people in urban areas. Held in London on 12 January 1996*. UNDP-World Bank Water and Sanitation Programme.

TAYLER, K. (1997a) Institutionalising Participation - Lessons from Pakistan, in Proceedings of 14th Inter-Schools Conference on Development, Edinburgh.

TAYLER, K. (1997b) When is Sewerage a Viable Sanitation Option? Unpublished report, GHK-RT, London, UK.

UNCHS (1993) The Urban Poor as Agents of Development: Community Action Planning in Sri Lanka, UNCHS, Nairobi

UNCHS/CityNet (1997) *Partnership for Local Action: A sourcebook on participatory approaches to shelter and human settlement improvement for local government officials*. UNCHS (Habitat), Community Development Programme for Asia, Thailand.

UNDP-World Bank Water and Sanitation Group RWSG - South Asia (1996) Proceedings of Workshop on Sanitation for Poor People in Urban Areas. Held in London on 12 January 1996. UNDP-World Bank Water and Sanitation Programme.

UNDP-World Bank Water and Sanitation Group RWSG - South Asia (1997) Regional Workshop on Sanitation for Low Income Urban Communities: Proceedings. UNDP-World Bank Water and Sanitation Programme, RWSG for South Asia, New Delhi, India.

UNDP-World Bank Water and Sanitation Programme (1997) 'Sanitation for the Urban Poor: The Strategic Sanitation Approach', in Simpson-Hebert, M., and Woods, S. (Eds.) *Sanitation Promotion Kit.* World Health Organisation, Switzerland.

VARLEY, R.C.G. (1997) 'Financing Low-Income Household Sanitation Facilities Through Household Credit' in Simpson-Hebert, M. and Woods, S. (Eds.) *Sanitation Promotion Kit.* World Health Organisation, Switzerland.

WATSON, G. (1995) Good Sewers Cheap? Agency-Customer Interactions in Low-Cost Urban Sanitation in Brazil, World Bank Water and Sanitation Division, Washington

WHITTINGTON et al (1992) Household Demand for Improved Sanitation Services: A case study of Kumasi, Ghana. The World Bank, Washington DC.

WHITTINGTON et al (1996) 'Implementing a Demand Driven Approach to Community Water Supply Planning: A Case Study of Lugazi, Uganda'. Forthcoming in *Water International,* 1998

WHITTINGTON, D. (1998) 'Administering Contingent Valuation Surveys in Developing Countries'. *World Development,* 26, 1, pp 21-30

WORLD BANK (1992) *World Development Report.* New York: Oxford University Press.

WORLD BANK / GOVERNMENT OF INDIA (1997) Workshop on Urban Water Supply and Sanitation: Draft Consultant's Report, volumes I and II Ministry of Urban Affairs and Employment, India

WORLD BANK WATER DEMAND RESEARCH TEAM (1993) 'Demand for Water in Rural Areas: Determinants and Policy Implications' *World Bank Res. Observer,* 8, 1, pp 47-70

WRIGHT, A.M. (1997) *Towards a Strategic Sanitation Approach: Improving the sustainability of urban sanitation in developing countries* UNDP-World Bank Water and Sanitation Programme Washington USA

WSSCC (1997) Demand Responsive Programming and Equity: A Discussion Paper for the Water Supply and Sanitation Sector. Collaborative Council

Working Group on Advocacy and Communication Strategies. IRC, The Netherlands.

WUNSCH, J.S. (1991) 'Sustaining Third World Infrastructure Investments: Decentralisation and Alternative Strategies'. *Public Administration and Development*, Vol. 11, pp 5-23

ZAIDI, A. (1997) The Rural Water Supply and Sanitation Sector in Pakistan: Policy, Institutions and Prospects, unpublished study commissioned by WaterAid.

Printed in the USA
CPSIA information can be obtained
at www.ICGtesting.com
JSHW012046140824
68134JS00034B/3280